2ND EDITION

THE **BIG BOOK** OF

PIANO · VOCAL · GUITAR

LOVE SONGS

ISBN 0-634-03405-7

HAL•LEONARD®
CORPORATION
7777 W. BLUEMOUND RD. P.O. BOX 13819 MILWAUKEE, WI 53213

Visit Hal Leonard Online at
www.halleonard.com

CONTENTS

ALL I ASK OF YOU

from THE PHANTOM OF THE OPERA

Music by ANDREW LLOYD WEBBER
Lyrics by CHARLES HART
Additional Lyrics by RICHARD STILGOE

No more talk of dark - ness, for - get these wide - eyed fears: I'm

here, noth - ing can harm you, my words will warm and calm you.

Let me be your free - dom, let day - light dry your tears: I'm

8

ALWAYS ON MY MIND

Words and Music by WAYNE THOMPSON,
MARK JAMES and JOHNNY CHRISTOPHER

Lyrics:

May-be I did-n't treat you _ quite as good _ as I should have.

May-be I did-n't hold you _ all those lone-ly, lone-ly times, _

May-be I did-n't love you _ quite as of-ten as I could have.

and I guess I nev-er told you _ I'm so hap-py that you're mine. _

(1.,3.) Lit-tle things I should have

(2.) If I made you feel _

10

AND I LOVE HER

Words and Music by JOHN LENNON
and PAUL McCARTNEY

BEAUTIFUL IN MY EYES

Words and Music by
JOSHUA KADISON

BEAUTY AND THE BEAST

from Walt Disney's BEAUTY AND THE BEAST

Lyrics by HOWARD ASHMAN
Music by ALAN MENKEN

BÉSAME MUCHO
(Kiss Me Much)

Music and Spanish Words by CONSUELO VELÁZQUEZ
English Words by SUNNY SKYLAR

Bé - sa - me, _____ bé - sa - me mu - cho, _____
Bé - sa - me, _____ bé - sa - me mu - cho, _____

each time I cling to your kiss I hear mu - sic di - vine. _____
co - mo si fue - ra es - ta no - che la úl - ti - ma vez; _____

Bé - sa - me mu - cho, _____
bé - sa - me mu - cho, _____

26

BODY AND SOUL

Words by EDWARD HEYMAN,
ROBERT SOUR and FRANK EYTON
Music by JOHN GREEN

CAN'T HELP LOVIN' DAT MAN

from SHOW BOAT

Lyrics by OSCAR HAMMERSTEIN II
Music by JEROME KERN

CHEEK TO CHEEK
from the RKO Radio Motion Picture TOP HAT

Words and Music by
IRVING BERLIN

CHERISH

Words and Music by
TERRY KIRKMAN

Cher-ish is the word I use to de-scribe _____
Per-ish is the word that more than ap-plies _____

all the feel-ing that I have hid-ing here for you in-side. _____
to the hope in my heart each time I re-a-lize _____

You don't know how man-y times I've wished that I had
that I am not gon-na be the one to share your

(They Long to Be)
CLOSE TO YOU

Lyric by HAL DAVID
Music by BURT BACHARACH

ENDLESS LOVE

from ENDLESS LOVE

Words and Music by
LIONEL RICHIE

Oh, _____ and _____ love, _____

(Everything I Do)
I DO IT FOR YOU

from the Motion Picture ROBIN HOOD: PRINCE OF THIEVES

Words and Music by BRYAN ADAMS,
ROBERT JOHN LANGE and MICHAEL KAMEN

way, __ yeah. __

Oh, you can't tell me it's not worth try - ing for. I can't

FIELDS OF GOLD

Music and Lyrics by
STING

Flowing, moderately

You'll re - mem - ber me, when the west wind moves _ up a -
stay with me, will you be my love _ a -

on the fields _ of bar - ley. You'll for - get the sun in his
mong the fields _ of bar - ley? We'll for - get the sun in his

THE FIRST TIME
EVER I SAW YOUR FACE

Words and Music by
EWAN MacCOLL

FLY ME TO THE MOON
(In Other Words)

Words and Music by
BART HOWARD

GOD ONLY KNOWS

Words and Music by BRIAN WILSON
and TONY ASHER

A GROOVY KIND OF LOVE

Words and Music by TONI WINE
and CAROLE BAYER SAGER

HERE AND NOW

Words and Music by TERRY STEELE
and DAVID ELLIOT

HERE, THERE AND EVERYWHERE

Words and Music by JOHN LENNON
and PAUL McCARTNEY

HOW DEEP IS THE OCEAN

(How High Is the Sky)

Words and Music by
IRVING BERLIN

HOW DEEP IS YOUR LOVE

from the Motion Picture SATURDAY NIGHT FEVER

Words and Music by ROBIN GIBB,
MAURICE GIBB and BARRY GIBB

I CAN'T MAKE YOU LOVE ME

Words and Music by MIKE REID
and ALLEN SHAMBLIN

94

I DON'T WANT TO WALK WITHOUT YOU

from the Paramount Picture SWEATER GIRL

Words by FRANK LOESSER
Music by JULE STYNE

Moderately

All our friends _ keep knock-ing at the door. They've

asked me out ___ a hun-dred times or more, but all I say ___ is:

"Leave me in the gloom," and here I stay _ with-in my lone-ly room. 'Cause,

I HONESTLY LOVE YOU

Words and Music by PETER ALLEN
and JEFF BARRY

May-be I hang a-round__ here a lit-tle more than I should; we
You don't__ have to an- swer; I see it in your eyes.

both know I got some- where else__ to go. But
May- be it was bet- ter left__ un- said. But

I LEFT MY HEART IN
SAN FRANCISCO

Words by DOUGLASS CROSS
Music by GEORGE CORY

I WANNA BE LOVED

Words by BILLY ROSE and EDWARD HEYMAN
Music by JOHN GREEN

112

I WILL WAIT FOR YOU
from THE UMBRELLAS OF CHERBOURG

Music by MICHEL LEGRAND
Original French Text by JACQUES DEMY
English Words by NORMAN GIMBEL

115

I WON'T LAST A DAY WITHOUT YOU

Words and Music by PAUL WILLIAMS
and ROGER NICHOLS

Day af-ter day __ I must face a world __ of strang-ers where I
So man-y times __ when the cit-y seems __ to be with-out a

don't be-long; __ I'm not that strong. It's nice to know __ that there's
friend-ly face, __ a lone-ly place, it's nice to know __ that you'll

some-one I __ can turn to, who will al-ways care; __ you're
be there if __ I need you, and you'll al-ways smile; __ it's

Vocal sung one octave lower than written.

I'LL BE THERE

Words and Music by BERRY GORDY,
HAL DAVIS, WILLIE HUTCH and BOB WEST

Just call my name _____ and I'll ___ be there. ___

1
C7sus

2
Freely
B♭ Gm7
Just call my name _____

B♭/C
___ and I'll ___ be there. ___

F
a tempo

E♭ B♭
F
E♭ B♭
molto rit.

I'LL BE

Words and Music by
EDWIN McCAIN

Original key: B Major. This edition has been transposed up one half-step to be more playable.

131

IF

Moderately, with feeling

Words and Music by
DAVID GATES

smoothly
mp

If a

pic - ture paints a thou - sand words, _ then why _

man could be two plac - es at ____ one time, _

ISN'T IT ROMANTIC?
from the Paramount Picture LOVE ME TONIGHT

Words by LORENZ HART
Music by RICHARD RODGERS

JUST THE WAY YOU ARE

Words and Music by
BILLY JOEL

144

IT COULD HAPPEN TO YOU

from the Paramount Picture AND THE ANGELS SING

Words by JOHNNY BURKE
Music by JAMES VAN HEUSEN

LADY

Words and Music by
LIONEL RICHIE

Moderately slow, with feeling

La - dy, _____ I'm your
La - dy, _____ for so

knight in shin-ing ar - mor and I love you, _____ you have made me what I
man - y years I thought I'd nev - er find you, _____ you have come in - to my

am and _____ I am yours. _____
life and _____ made me whole. _____ For -

LADY IN RED

Words and Music by
CHRIS DeBURGH

Moderately slow

LET IT BE ME
(Je T'appartiens)

English Words by MANN CURTIS
French Words by PIERRE DeLANOE
Music by GILBERT BECAUD

THE LOOK OF LOVE

from CASINO ROYALE

Words by HAL DAVID
Music by BURT BACHARACH

Medium Rock Ballad (with much feeling)

LOVE ME WITH ALL YOUR HEART
(Cuando Calienta el Sol)

Original Words and Music by CARLOS RIGUAL
and CARLOS A. MARTINOLI
English Words by SUNNY SKYLAR

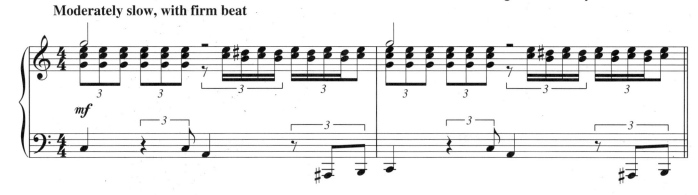

Moderately slow, with firm beat

Love me with all your heart, ___ that's all I want, love; ___
Cuan - do ca - lien - ta el sol ___ a - quí en la pla - ya, ___

Love me with all of your heart or not at all; ___
sien - to tu cuer - po vi - brar cer - ca de mí, ___

MORE THAN WORDS

Words and Music by NUNO BETTENCOURT
and GARY CHERONE

Say - in' "I ___ love ___ you" is
Now that I've ___ tried ___ to

not the words ___ I want ___ to ___ hear ___ from you. ___ It's not that I ___
talk to you ___ and make ___ you ___ un - der - stand, ___ all ___ you ___

Original key: F♯ major. This edition has been transposed up one half-step to be more playable.

MY FUNNY VALENTINE

from BABES IN ARMS

Words by LORENZ HART
Music by RICHARD RODGERS

MY GIRL

Words and Music by WILLIAM "SMOKEY" ROBINSON
and RONALD WHITE

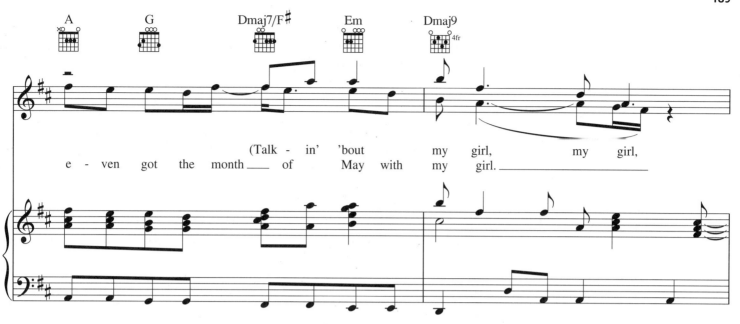

(Talk - in' 'bout my girl, my girl,
e - ven got the month _ of May with my girl. _____

my girl, whoa _____ whoa.) _____
Talk - in' 'bout, _____ talk - in' 'bout, talk - in' 'bout _ my _ girl. _

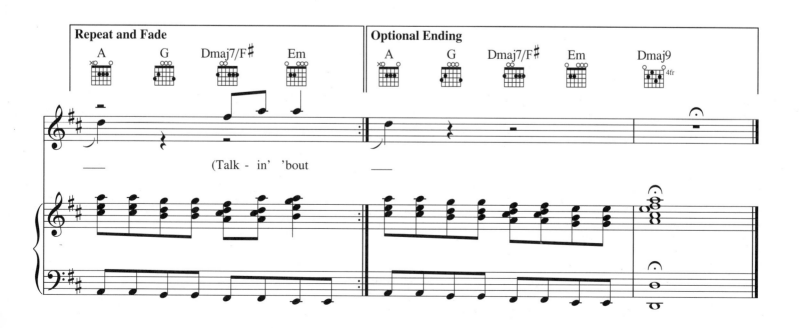

Repeat and Fade

Optional Ending

_____ (Talk - in' 'bout

MY HEART WILL GO ON
(Love Theme from 'Titanic')
from the Paramount and Twentieth Century Fox Motion Picture TITANIC

Music by JAMES HORNER
Lyric by WILL JENNINGS

MY LOVE

Words and Music by
PAUL and LINDA McCARTNEY

THE NEARNESS OF YOU

from the Paramount Picture ROMANCE IN THE DARK

Words by NED WASHINGTON
Music by HOAGY CARMICHAEL

MY ROMANCE
from JUMBO

Words by LORENZ HART
Music by RICHARD RODGERS

NOBODY LOVES ME LIKE YOU DO

Words by PAMELA PHILLIPS
Music by JAMES P. DUNNE

Female: Like a can - dle burn - ing bright,

love is glow - ing in ___ your eyes. ___

PUT YOUR HEAD ON MY SHOULDER

Words and Music by
PAUL ANKA

ON THE WINGS OF LOVE

Words and Music by JEFFREY OSBORNE
and PETER SCHLESS

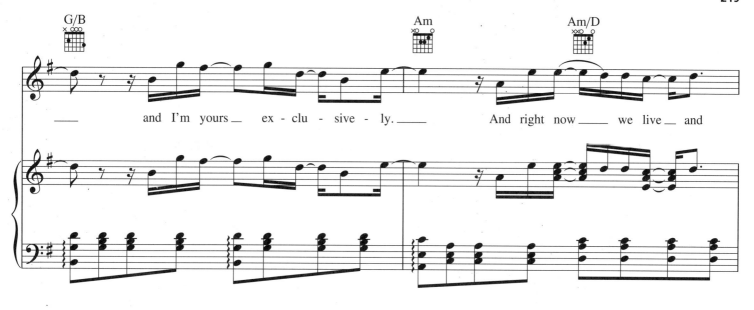

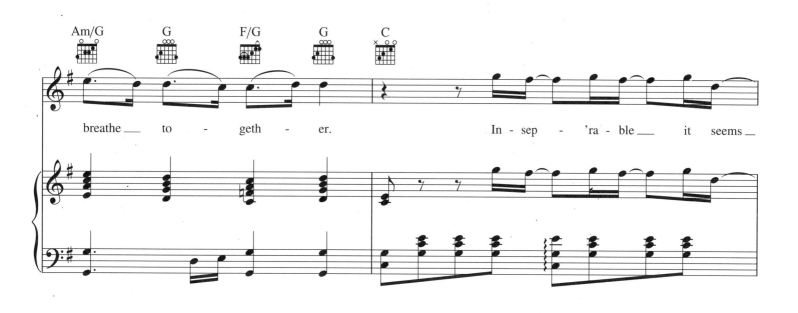

ONLY YOU
(And You Alone)

Words and Music by BUCK RAM
and ANDE RAND

Slowly, with feeling

Only You____ can make this world seem right,____
You____ can make this world change in me,____
Only You____ for it's true,____ can make the
you are my
dark - ness bright.____ On - ly You and you, a -
des - ti - ny.____ When you hold my hand, I

THE POWER OF LOVE

Words by MARY SUSAN APPLEGATE and JENNIFER RUSH
Music by CANDY DEROUGE and GUNTHER MENDE

229

PRECIOUS AND FEW

Words and Music by
WALTER D. NIMS

RIBBON IN THE SKY

Words and Music by
STEVIE WONDER

Oh, so

SAVE THE BEST FOR LAST

Words and Music by PHIL GALDSTON,
JON LIND and WENDY WALDMAN

242

Just when I thought ____ our chance ____ had passed, ____

you go and save ____ the best ____ for last. ____

All of the nights ____

SAVING ALL MY LOVE FOR YOU

Words by GERRY GOFFIN
Music by MICHAEL MASSER

SOME ENCHANTED EVENING

from SOUTH PACIFIC

Lyrics by OSCAR HAMMERSTEIN II
Music by RICHARD RODGERS

SEPTEMBER SONG
from the Musical Play KNICKERBOCKER HOLIDAY

Words by MAXWELL ANDERSON
Music by KURT WEILL

SOMEDAY

from Walt Disney's THE HUNCHBACK OF NOTRE DAME

Music by ALAN MENKEN
Lyrics by STEPHEN SCHWARTZ

SOMETHING

Words and Music by
GEORGE HARRISON

SOMETIMES WHEN WE TOUCH

Words by DAN HILL
Music by BARRY MANN

270

A SUNDAY KIND OF LOVE

Words and Music by BARBARA BELLE, LOUIS PRIMA,
ANITA LEONARD and STAN RHODES

TAKE MY BREATH AWAY
(Love Theme)
from the Paramount Picture TOP GUN

Words and Music by GIORGIO MORODER
and TOM WHITLOCK

THREE TIMES A LADY

Words and Music by
LIONEL RICHIE

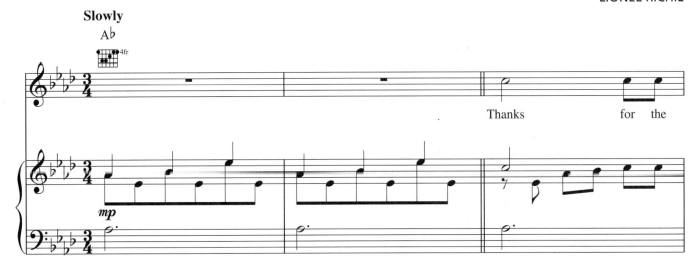

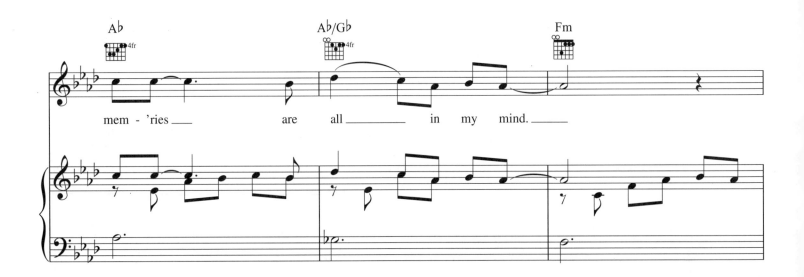

TRULY

Words and Music by
LIONEL RICHIE

TWO SLEEPY PEOPLE

from the Paramount Motion Picture THANKS FOR THE MEMORY

Words by FRANK LOESSER
Music by HOAGY CARMICHAEL

UNCHAINED MELODY

from the Motion Picture UNCHAINED

Lyric by HY ZARET
Music by ALEX NORTH

Tempo I

UNTIL IT'S TIME FOR YOU TO GO

Words and Music by
BUFFY SAINTE-MARIE

Slow Waltz

UP WHERE WE BELONG

from the Paramount Picture AN OFFICER AND A GENTLEMAN

Words by WILL JENNINGS
Music by BUFFY SAINTE-MARIE and JACK NITZSCHE

VALENTINE

Words and Music by JACK KUGELL
and JIM BRICKMAN

THE WAY YOU LOOK TONIGHT
from SWING TIME

Words by DOROTHY FIELDS
Music by JEROME KERN

WE'VE ONLY JUST BEGUN

Words and Music by ROGER NICHOLS
and PAUL WILLIAMS

WHAT THE WORLD NEEDS NOW IS LOVE

Lyric by HAL DAVID
Music by BURT BACHARACH

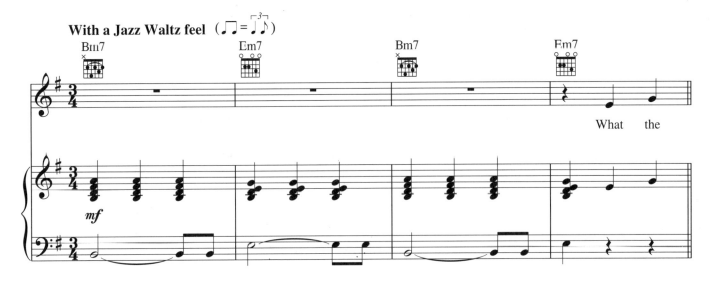

WHEN I FALL IN LOVE

from ONE MINUTE TO ZERO

Words by EDWARD HEYMAN
Music by VICTOR YOUNG

323

WHEN YOU SAY NOTHING AT ALL

Words and Music by PAUL OVERSTREET
and DON SCHLITZ

Moderately slow

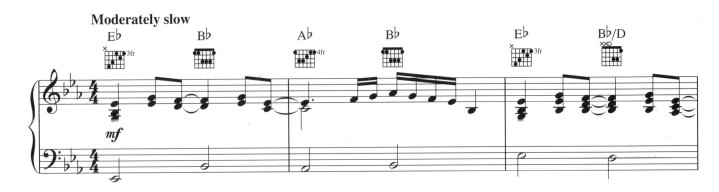

It's a-maz-ing how you can speak right to my heart.
All day long I can hear peo-ple talk-ing out loud,

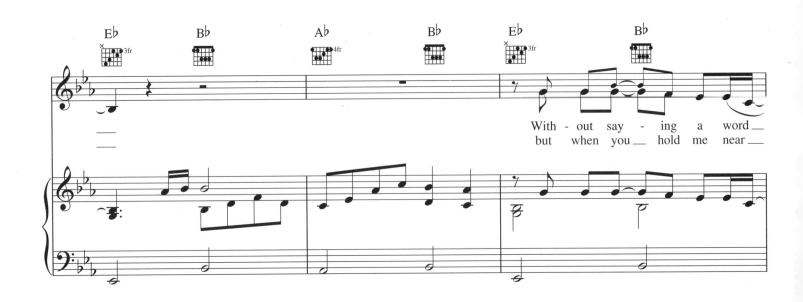

With-out say-ing a word
but when you hold me near

truth in your eyes ___ say - ing you'll ___ nev - er leave ___ me. A

touch of your hand ___ says you'll catch ___ me if ev - er I fall. ___

Now you say it best ___ when you say noth - ing at all. _

when you say noth-ing at all. _____

The

D.S. al Coda

CODA

when you say noth-ing at all. ____

rit.

WHERE DO I BEGIN
(Love Theme)
from the Paramount Picture LOVE STORY

Words by CARL SIGMAN
Music by FRANCIS LAI

Where do I be-gin _____ to tell the sto-ry of how
With her first hel-lo _____ she gave a mean-ing to this

great a love can be, _____ the sweet love sto-ry that is
emp-ty world of mine. _____ There'd nev-er be an-oth-er

old-er than the sea, the sim-ple truth a-bout the
love, an-oth-er time; she came in-to my life and

hours in a day? I have no an-swers now, but this much I can say:

I know I'll need her till the stars all burn a-way, and she'll be

there.

A WHOLE NEW WORLD
(Aladdin's Theme)
from Walt Disney's ALADDIN

Music by ALAN MENKEN
Lyrics by TIM RICE

WONDERFUL TONIGHT

Words and Music by
ERIC CLAPTON

339

341

YOU LIGHT UP MY LIFE

Words and Music by
JOSEPH BROOKS

YOU'VE GOT A FRIEND

Words and Music by
CAROLE KING

*Vocal harmony sung 2nd time only

WITHDRAWN
Big Books of Music

Our "Big Books" feature big selections of popular titles under one cover, perfect for performing musicians, music aficionados or the serious hobbyist. All books are arranged for piano, voice, and guitar, and feature stay-open binding, so the books lie flat without breaking the spine.

BIG BOOK OF BALLADS
63 songs.
00310485 ....$19.95

BIG BOOK OF BIG BAND HITS
84 songs.
00310701 ....$19.95

BIG BOOK OF BROADWAY
70 songs.
00311658 ....$19.95

BIG BOOK OF CHILDREN'S SONGS
55 songs.
00359261 ....$14.95

GREAT BIG BOOK OF CHILDREN'S SONGS
76 songs.
00310002 ....$14.95

MIGHTY BIG BOOK OF CHILDREN'S SONGS
67 songs.
00310467 ....$14.95

REALLY BIG BOOK OF CHILDREN'S SONGS
63 songs.
00310372 ....$15.95

BIG BOOK OF CHILDREN'S MOVIE SONGS
66 songs.
00310731 ....$17.95

BIG BOOK OF CHRISTMAS SONGS
126 songs.
00311520 ....$19.95

BIG BOOK OF CLASSIC ROCK
77 songs.
00310801 ....$19.95

BIG BOOK OF CLASSICAL MUSIC
100 songs.
00310508 ....$19.95

BIG BOOK OF CONTEMPORARY CHRISTIAN FAVORITES
50 songs.
00310021 ....$19.95

BIG BOOK OF COUNTRY MUSIC
64 songs.
00310188 ....$19.95

BIG BOOK OF DISCO & FUNK
70 songs.
00310878 ....$19.95

BIG BOOK OF EARLY ROCK N' ROLL
99 songs.
00310398 ....$19.95

BIG BOOK OF GOLDEN OLDIES
73 songs.
00310756 ....$19.95

BIG BOOK OF GOSPEL SONGS
100 songs.
00310604 ....$19.95

BIG BOOK OF HYMNS
125 hymns.
00310510 ....$17.95

BIG BOOK OF IRISH SONGS
76 songs.
00310981 ....$16.95

BIG BOOK OF JAZZ
75 songs.
00311557 ....$19.95

BIG BOOK OF LATIN AMERICAN SONGS
89 songs.
00311562 ....$19.95

BIG BOOK OF LOVE SONGS
80 songs.
00310784 ....$19.95

BIG BOOK OF MOTOWN
84 songs.
00311061 ....$19.95

BIG BOOK OF MOVIE MUSIC
72 songs.
00311582 ....$19.95

BIG BOOK OF NOSTALGIA
158 songs.
00310004 ....$19.95

BIG BOOK OF RHYTHM & BLUES
67 songs.
00310169 ....$19.95

BIG BOOK OF ROCK
78 songs.
00311566 ....$19.95

BIG BOOK OF SOUL
71 songs.
00310771 ....$19.95

BIG BOOK OF STANDARDS
86 songs.
00311667 ....$19.95

BIG BOOK OF SWING
84 songs.
00310359 ....$19.95

BIG BOOK OF TORCH SONGS
75 songs.
00310561 ....$19.95

BIG BOOK OF TV THEME SONGS
78 songs.
00310504 ....$19.95

BIG BOOK OF WEDDING MUSIC
77 songs.
00311567 ....$19.95

FOR MORE INFORMATION, SEE YOUR LOCAL MUSIC DEALER, OR WRITE TO:

HAL•LEONARD®
CORPORATION
7777 W. BLUEMOUND RD. P.O. BOX 13819 MILWAUKEE, WI 53213

Prices, contents, and availability subject to change without notice.

Visit **www.halleonard.com**
for our entire catalog and to view our complete songlists.